YOU CHOOSE BOOKS™

THE CIVIL WAR

An Interactive History Adventure

by Matt Doeden

Consultant:
Mark Snell, PhD
Associate Professor of History/Director
George Tyler Moore Center for the Study of the Civil War
Shepherd University
Shepherdstown, West Virginia

Capstone press®

Mankato, Minnesota

You Choose Books are published by Capstone Press,
151 Good Counsel Drive, P.O. Box 669, Mankato, Minnesota 56002.
www.capstonepub.com

062010
005844

Library of Congress Cataloging-in-Publication Data
Doeden, Matt.
    The Civil War: an interactive history adventure / by Matt Doeden.
    p. cm. — (You choose books. History)
    Includes bibliographical references and index.
    Summary: "Describes the people and events of the Civil War. The reader's choices reveal the
historical details from the perspective of a Union soldier at Gettysburg, a civilian during the siege
of Vicksburg, or a Confederate soldier at Chancellorsville" — Provided by publisher.
    ISBN 978-1-4296-3419-9 (library binding)
    ISBN 978-1-4296-3910-1 (softcover)
    ISBN 978-1-4296-5977-2 (saddle-stitched)
    1. United States — History — Civil War, 1861–1865 — Juvenile literature. I. Title.
E468.D635 2010
973.7 — dc22   2008055958

Editorial Credits
Angie Kaelberer, editor; Juliette Peters, set designer; Veronica Bianchini, book designer;
    Kim Brown, illustrator; Wanda Winch, media researcher

Photo Credits
The Art Archive/Massachusetts Commandery Military Order of the Loyal Legion and the
US Army Military History Institute, 59; Art Resource, N.Y./© The Metropolitan Museum
of Art, 33; Bridgeman Art Library/© Chicago History Museum, USA/A Confederate
Scout of General Turner Ashby at the Valley near Luray and New Hacket, Collins, J.A., 12;
Bridgeman Art Library/© Look and Learn/Private Collection/General Grant meets Robert
E. Lee, 104; Bridgeman Art Library/© Look and Learn/Private Collection/The Siege of
Vicksburg, McBride, Angus, 70; Chamberlain and the 20th Maine by Mort Künstler, ©1993
Mort Künstler, Inc., www.mkunstler.com, 42; Classic Portraits in Oil/Noel Pantig, 86; Corbis/
Bettmann, 6; Corbis/Royalty-Free, 100, 103; Gallon Historical Art, Inc., www.gallon.com
(Texas Pride), 51; Getty Images Inc./Hulton Archive/MPI, 73, 94; The Glorious Fourth by
Mort Künstler, ©1989 Mort Künstler, Inc., www.mkunstler.com, 98; Library of Congress/Prints
and Photographs Division, 9, 39, 57; North Wind Picture Archives, 17; Old Court House
Museum, Vicksburg, Mississippi, 82; Paintings by Don Troiani, www.historicalimagebank.com,
cover, 19, 24, 26, 52, 64, 67; Used with permission of Documenting the American South, The
University of North Carolina at Chapel Hill Libraries, 79; www.printroom.com, 34

This book focuses on three events of the Civil War that took place during 1863. The four years
of war also included many other pivotal events not described in this book.

TABLE OF CONTENTS

About Your Adventure

YOU are living in the United States in 1863. A civil war between the North and the South has divided the nation. Which side will you support? What decisions will you have to make?

In this book, you'll explore how the choices people made meant the difference between life and death. The events you'll experience happened to real people.

Chapter One sets the scene. Then you choose which path to read. Follow the directions at the bottom of each page. The choices you make will change your outcome. After you finish one path, go back and read the others for new perspectives and more adventures.

YOU CHOOSE the path
you take through history.

Confederate soldiers bombarded Fort Sumter from Fort Moultrie on April 12, 1861.

A NATION DIVIDED

The year is 1863. The United States and the Confederate States of America are in the middle of a bitter civil war. The war started April 12, 1861, when Confederate soldiers fired on Fort Sumter in South Carolina. Since then, the Yankee troops of the North and the Rebels of the South have fought many battles.

The issues behind the war are complicated. But you understand a few things. The South wants its independence from the North. The 11 states of the Confederacy have seceded, or withdrawn, from the United States. They want their freedom from what they see as a controlling federal government.

Turn the page.

Slavery is a central issue. Slavery is illegal in the North. Southern states want to keep the right to own slaves. On January 1, 1863, President Abraham Lincoln signed the Emancipation Proclamation. This order freed slaves living in Confederate-held areas. The North's main goal is to keep the Union together, but it also supports ending slavery in the entire country.

In the East, the Confederate army has dominated the first two years of the war. Under the leadership of Generals Robert E. Lee, Joseph Johnston, Thomas "Stonewall" Jackson, James Longstreet, and others, the Confederacy has won battle after battle. President Abraham Lincoln knows the Union needs a big victory. But he struggles to find a leader who can match up to the Confederate commander, Lee.

In the South, slaves were held in slave pens like this one before they were sold.

The situation is a little brighter for the Union in the West. Early battles focused on control of Tennessee, Missouri, and Kentucky. Although Missouri and Kentucky are slave states, they decided to stay in the Union. Even so, both states have troops who fight for the Confederacy.

Turn the page.

In April 1862, Confederate forces in the West suffered a major blow. At the bloody Battle of Shiloh in Tennessee, General Ulysses S. Grant led the Union to victory. During the battle, General Albert Sidney Johnson was killed. He commanded the Confederate forces in the West. Soon after, Union forces captured the important Mississippi River cities of Memphis, Tennessee, and New Orleans, Louisiana.

General Grant's next goal is complete control of the Mississippi River. In spring 1863, he moves his army toward the port city of Vicksburg, Mississippi. His action forces Confederate troops to retreat into the city.

By this time, the war seems to be at a turning point. If the Confederates continue their success in the East, the end may be near. But the Union army still outnumbers the Confederate forces. A few victories could quickly turn the tide and bring the Confederate army to its knees.

❧ To join the Confederate army at Chancellorsville, turn to page **13**.

❧ To join the Union army at Gettysburg, turn to page **43**.

❧ To live as a civilian during the Union siege of Vicksburg, turn to page **71**.

Civil War army scouts and cavalry gathered information about the enemy's location and battle plans.

CHAPTER 2

A CONFEDERATE AT CHANCELLORSVILLE

It is the evening of April 30, 1863, in the Confederate army's camp near Fredericksburg, Virginia. Groups of men gather to play cards or dice, their laughter rising up over the camp.

You can't join in the fun just yet. You and your friend, Charles, are part of a scouting unit. Your job is to keep track of Union General Joseph Hooker's army.

You and Charles stand before General Thomas "Stonewall" Jackson and his aides. Jackson listens intently as you describe the land you've scouted. He's especially interested in any roads that run west just to the south of the Union line.

13

Turn the page.

"Hooker has at least 50,000 men camped near Chancellorsville, sir, and probably more on the way," you tell Jackson.

"Chancellorsville! Is that a town?" Jackson asks. "No, sir," Charles answers. "It's the Chancellor family's farmhouse. It's at the intersection of several roads along the Orange Turnpike, about 11 miles west of Fredericksburg."

Jackson nods slowly and dismisses you. "Get some sleep, men," he adds. "That's an order."

As the two of you walk away, you sigh with relief. Jackson is a gruff and intimidating man. Only General Robert E. Lee commands more respect from the men.

The Confederate army is confident. They've whipped the Union again and again. Now the largest armies of the Union and the Confederacy are moving closer. The outcome of the war could soon be decided.

CHANCELLORSVILLE BATTLEFIELD

Building	🏠
City	●
River	〰️
Road	—

"Come on," Charles says. "I know where we can get in on a poker game."

"You go ahead," you say. Tomorrow, Lee will split his forces — a huge risk. Whether you go with Stonewall Jackson to attack the Union flank or stay with the main army, you want to be rested.

❧ To stay with the main force, turn to page **16**.

❧ To march with Stonewall Jackson, turn to page **18**.

About 2:00 the next morning, May 1, Jackson marches off with about 30,000 men. They quietly move toward the Union left flank.

After Jackson's forces leave, you get a few more hours of sleep. As dawn breaks, you and Charles ride north, searching for any movement along the Yankee line.

Suddenly, you notice movement in the distance. "What was that?" you ask.

"I'm not sure," Charles replies. "Let's go look."

You ride toward a small, tree-covered ridge. You spot three people huddled behind some bushes. As you ride closer, you see their dark skin and ragged clothing. You realize that they're runaway slaves.

"You there," you say, drawing your revolver. "Come out."

Escaped slaves moved during the night and hid during the day.

A woman and two children emerge, looking terrified. "Please, sir, don't turn us in," the woman begs. "They'll whip me and punish the children."

You feel sorry for the slaves, but you are an officer in the Confederate army. Letting these people go would be a crime. You could be put in prison for helping them escape.

➤ To report the slaves, turn to page **21**.

➤ To let them go, turn to page **22**.

Long before dawn the next morning, May 1, you're back on your horse. Charles is at your side. The two of you are scouting ahead of Jackson's force of about 30,000 men. General Lee has sent him to attack the Union army near Chancellorsville. About 10,000 troops remain at the camp.

Later that morning, you reach Tabernacle Church, about 6 miles east of Chancellorsville. About 16,000 troops under the command of Confederate Generals Dick Anderson and Lafayette McLaws are digging trenches. Jackson orders these troops to join his forces. The combined forces continue marching. By nightfall, the troops are camped about 2 miles south of Chancellorsville. General Lee joins them.

Lee (center, left) and Jackson (center, right) met early the morning of May 2 to plan the attack.

Before dawn the next morning, Charles shakes you awake. "We're moving again," he says. "General Jackson's marching roundabout through the woods to stay undercover. He's planning to attack the Yankees by surprise."

By 7:30, you're back on the road. General Lee remains at the camp with Anderson and McLaws' troops. Behind you, Jackson's soldiers march in near silence.

Turn the page.

The march goes smoothly, except for an attack by Union soldiers at the rear of the column. But Hooker seems to think that the Confederate soldiers are retreating. By late afternoon, Jackson's troops are in position just outside the Union camp. They're hidden in an area of thick, tangled trees and brush called the Wilderness.

You stand by Jackson as he makes his final preparations. The men will charge at the unsuspecting Yankees from the cover of the trees. Jackson will need good officers by his side. He'll also need as many soldiers as possible to carry out the attack. Where will you serve?

↠ *To join the lines, turn to page* **24**.

↠ *To stay by Jackson's side, turn to page* **26**.

The law is the law. What happens to these people is out of your hands. "Charles, over here!" you shout. The two of you march the slaves back to a nearby farm. The owner thanks you and tells you the runaways will be punished.

When you return to camp, Lee's troops are preparing to launch several attacks. Lee hopes to keep the Union army's attention from Jackson's force. You and Charles head north with a small group. You work your way through an area of thick trees and brush called the Wilderness.

You fire a few shots at a weak point in the Union line. As the Yankees return fire, you start to retreat. You see a Union general not far ahead. You could shoot him. But you'd have to get closer, and your mission is already complete.

➻ *To shoot the general, turn to page* **36**.

➻ *To return to camp, turn to page* **37**.

What can you do? Turning in the slaves would be wrong, and you know it. With a deep breath, you make your decision.

"There's a large Yankee force north of here," you whisper. "Hurry. Get behind the lines to freedom."

"Thank you, sir," the woman sobs.

You hesitate and add, "If you get caught, don't tell anyone that I saw you."

"Too late for that, I'm afraid," you hear from behind you. You turn and see Charles. His pistol is drawn. It's pointed at you.

"What are you doing?" your voice cracks.

"You're helping fugitives," Charles spits. "You're betraying the Confederacy." Charles edges closer, his weapon still pointed at your chest.

"You don't have to do this," you beg.

"We'll let a court-martial decide what to do with you," Charles replies.

You don't know what to do. If you go with Charles, you might be put in prison. The slaves will be returned to their owner, where they'll suffer for their escape attempt. But the only other choice is to attack Charles and attempt to get away.

➼ To defend yourself and try to escape, turn to page **30**.

➼ To do as you're told, turn to page **32**.

Confederate soldiers moved quietly through the Wilderness toward the Union camp.

You take a position along the front lines, eager to be part of the charge. It's suppertime, and you can smell bacon and potatoes frying in the Yankee camp. You've had little to eat since the march began, and your mouth waters.

Finally, the order comes. You and your fellow soldiers burst out of the woods, letting out your famous Rebel yell. The Yankees are caught completely off guard. They scatter, desperately trying to form lines of defense.

A haze of smoke rolls across the battlefield as the Confederate troops advance. The sound of gunfire fills the air. Horses try to flee from the noise. The Yankees finally organize a defense, but it's too late. You scream and cheer as you help lead a charge at the main Union line.

In the distance, you see Yankee soldiers getting ready to fire a cannon into the Confederate line. The cannon is pointed in your direction!

⇢ *To charge at the cannon, turn to page **34**.*

⇢ *To take cover, turn to page **38**.*

Union soldiers tried to organize a defense against the surprise attack.

You stay with Jackson and his aides as he orders the attack. Together, you watch as the Confederate troops storm out of the woods. The Yankees are caught by surprise as the loud Rebel yell rings out over the field. The Union soldiers desperately try to organize themselves and form a defense. A few succeed, but most aren't able to get ready in time.

The attack is fast and furious. "Press forward!" Jackson shouts. The Yankees turn and run for their lives. They leave rifles, equipment, and dead and wounded soldiers behind them.

As the sun sets, Jackson's troops chase the Yankees until the growing darkness stops them in their tracks. Some soldiers remain along the Orange Plank Road to watch for Yankee scouts or straggling soldiers.

You figure that Jackson will be pleased with the huge victory. Instead, he seems annoyed that the Union has until morning to regroup. Despite the darkness, Jackson wants to ride forward, closer to the lines.

❧ *To go with Jackson, turn to page **28**.*
❧ *To stay with the men guarding the road, turn to page **29**.*

You ride on the Orange Plank Road behind the general and his aides. Jackson is eager to continue pressing the Yankee line.

You can hear Union soldiers ahead. "It's not safe for you here, General," cautions one of Jackson's aides. Reluctantly, the general agrees. You turn your horses and make your way back toward your line. As you cross Old Mountain Road, you sense movement ahead of you. But before you can call out, gunfire follows. A man to your left slumps and falls from his horse.

"Cease firing!" shouts someone in your group. "You're firing into your own men!"

You realize what has happened. The soldiers guarding the road have confused your group for Yankee cavalry. You leap from your horse.

Turn to page 40.

You stay back as the general and his aides ride forward. You join a small group of guards who are watching the Orange Plank Road for Yankee scouts.

Trees are all around your position, making it even harder to see. After a little while, you hear muffled voices and the sound of horses approaching. Dark figures emerge ahead. Are they friends or enemies?

You're not sure what to do. If Yankees are approaching, you have to fire before they fire at you. But you're not sure who or what you'd be firing at in the darkness.

While you're thinking, one of the guards in your group fires a shot. Other guards follow his lead.

→ *To join in the firing, turn to page* **39**.

→ *To wait to shoot, turn to page* **40**.

You have just one chance. You turn to the slaves huddled in the brush and shout, "Run!" Then you lunge toward Charles, launching yourself from your horse's back. You knock the pistol from his hand.

Charles' horse rears back in surprise, throwing him to the ground. You quickly kick away his weapon and point your gun at him.

"Get down on the ground," you shout. You look back and see the woman and children running toward the north.

"You'll go to prison for this," Charles growls. "You can never return to the army. You'll be a deserter and a fugitive."

"If I kill you, nobody will ever know," you reply coldly. But even as you say the words, you know that you could never go through with it.

Charles is right. You can't go back. You have no choice but to desert the army.

You climb back onto your horse, your gun still pointed at Charles. You grab the reins of Charles' horse and lead it away. It'll take Charles hours to get back to the main army. The extra time will give you a head start.

You ride west. You know you can never go home now. You might go to Kansas or even to Texas. It will be a long, difficult ride. But you decide it's your best chance for a new life.

THE END

To follow another path, turn to page 11.
To read the conclusion, turn to page 101.

Your shoulders slump as you make your decision. Charles takes your weapon and marches the slaves back to a nearby farm. Then he leads you back to camp.

Charles tells General Lee what happened. Lee looks disappointed, but he says that he needs every man, including you, for the battle. He's planning several small attacks on the Union line. Lee wants to keep the enemy's attention away from Jackson's troops. Lee needs more information about the Union line, so he sends you to get a better look.

You ride carefully, staying under the cover of the Wilderness. Smoke in the distance tells you that you're getting close to the Union army.

Suddenly, you hear a snap from behind you. You spin around. Three Union soldiers stand with their guns pointed at you.

The Union captured about 462,000 Confederate soldiers during the war.

"Get down," one of them orders. You throw down your weapon and climb off your horse. The men march you into the Union camp. You'll be questioned and sent to a Union prison. If the Confederacy is going to win the war, it will have to do it without you.

THE END

To follow another path, turn to page 11.
To read the conclusion, turn to page 101.

Wounded soldiers awaited treatment near the battlefields.

With your sharp bayonet fixed to the front of your rifle, you charge at the Yankee troops who are firing the cannon. They see you coming, but it's too late. You crash into one soldier, the blade of your bayonet plunging deep into his stomach.

Another Yankee raises a pistol at you. You smash the butt of your rifle into his face, and he slumps to the ground. By this time, your fellow soldiers have noticed what's happening. Charles and another soldier race over, firing. A third Yankee falls to the ground.

As you turn to rejoin the battle, you hear a small click. Too late, you realize what it is. The man you stuck with the bayonet is clutching a pistol. You dive for cover just as he takes the shot. It catches you in the left shoulder. You cry out in pain as Charles shoots and kills the Yankee. You try to stand, but Charles stops you.

"Stay there," he says. "The Yankees are falling back. We'll get you help."

You lay there as the battle rages on. Your wound is painful, but you don't think your life is in danger. The battle will likely be a victory for your side, and you're proud of the role you played.

35

THE END

To follow another path, turn to page 11.
To read the conclusion, turn to page 101.

This could be a big opportunity. As the other men begin to fall back, you dash forward. Soon the general is within range. But the Yankees have spotted you as well. You dive to the ground and prepare to shoot. But Union troops quickly surround the general and raise their rifles.

Several shots whiz over your head, barely missing. You turn to run, but as you stand, you feel a sharp stinging in your left leg. The leg gives out, and you crash back down to the ground.

Seeing you down, several Union soldiers charge. You turn and raise your weapon. Bam! You're hit again, this time in the chest. Your weapon falls from your grasp as blackness closes in around your eyes. You've given your life for the Confederacy.

THE END

To follow another path, turn to page 11.
To read the conclusion, turn to page 101.

You've completed your mission. There's no need to risk your life. The important thing is that Jackson's forces succeed against the Union flank.

"Fall back!" you shout. The small group of soldiers makes its way back to the camp. That evening, you learn that Lee and Jackson's plan worked. The Confederacy won the day's battle. But there isn't much celebrating in the camp. Word comes that Jackson has been shot.

The battle continues for the next three days. Finally, on May 6, General Hooker retreats for the last time. On May 10, Jackson dies. You helped win a major battle, but the price was huge. You hope the Confederacy can still win the war without one of its finest generals.

THE END

To follow another path, turn to page 11.
To read the conclusion, turn to page 101.

"Get down!" you shout. You dive to the ground, holding your hands over your head.

When you look up, you realize you're the only one on the ground. Two other Confederate soldiers are charging the Yankee cannon. You feel ashamed. You leap to your feet to join the charge.

You raise your rifle and start to run toward the cannon. You hear what sounds like a boom of thunder. In an instant, you're thrown to the ground. Pain surges through your body. When you look down, your right leg is gone.

You hear the groans of several men nearby. You feel very cold. And you can't really feel the pain anymore. As your eyes slowly close, you know you won't be waking up again.

THE END

To follow another path, turn to page 11.
To read the conclusion, turn to page 101.

General Stonewall Jackson was shot accidentally by his fellow troops.

You raise your rifle and join in the fire. Several men in the other group fall to the ground.

"Cease firing! You're firing into your own men!" you hear. "General Jackson is hit in three places," someone else shouts.

You stand there in a daze while others rush to help the fallen general. What if your bullet was one of the shots that hit Jackson?

Turn to page **41**.

After the shooting stops, you see several men gathered around a figure lying on the ground. With horror, you realize that it's General Jackson. He's been hit once in his right hand and twice in his left arm.

"Get a stretcher!" you shout. "The general is hit!"

You turn to Jackson. "Are you hurt badly, sir?" you ask.

"I fear my arm is broken," he replies.

A doctor and one of Jackson's aides bandage his wounds. You feel helpless as Jackson is loaded onto a stretcher and carried away. Now all you can do is pray that Jackson will be all right.

The battle continues for three more days. On May 6, Hooker's army retreats across the Rappahannock River. The Confederates have scored a major victory.

At first, doctors believe General Jackson will recover. But he develops pneumonia and dies on May 10. His death is a terrible blow to the Confederacy.

You and Charles see General Lee later that day. He's always been strong and confident, but you can tell Jackson's death has shaken him badly. "Let's go," Charles says as you watch Lee ride away. "This war won't end for one man."

The two of you ride off. You know you'll keep fighting to honor your country and preserve your way of life.

THE END

To follow another path, turn to page 11.
To read the conclusion, turn to page 101.

Colonel Joshua Chamberlain (front) led the 20th Maine Infantry into battle.

THREE DAYS IN GETTYSBURG

It is July 1, 1863. Night has fallen over the countryside. You've been marching for days in the Maryland and Pennsylvania heat, so you're grateful for the cooler night air. Your tattered Union army uniform is soaked in sweat and covered in dirt.

You're a private serving under Colonel Joshua Chamberlain in the Union Army of the Potomac. Your regiment, the 20th Maine Infantry, is marching to a little town called Gettysburg, Pennsylvania. There, the main armies of the Union and the Confederacy have met to battle. The fighting began early this morning.

Turn the page.

As your regiment comes around a bend in the road, you're ordered to stop. You are several miles from Gettysburg. You see a few large wooded ridges and hills that dot the flat landscape.

"That's it?" asks George, your closest friend. "Seems like a strange place to fight a battle that may decide the war." You nod, too tired to talk.

You've heard this will be a big battle. General George Meade, the new Union commander, will make his stand against Confederate General Robert E. Lee. Failure to drive back the Rebels could leave the U.S. capital, Washington, D.C., at risk of being captured.

The next afternoon, July 2, the heavy fighting begins. Your regiment is placed at the far end of the Union line. You're defending a wooded hill called Little Round Top. You and the other soldiers take cover behind boulders and trees.

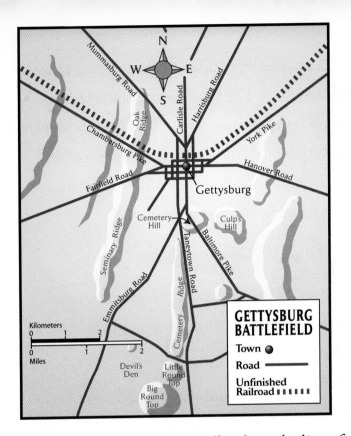

Colonel Chamberlain walks along the line of troops. He looks over the men as he strokes his long mustache. "The Rebels will attack the hill soon," he says. "The high ground will give us the advantage. We cannot fall back. If we fail, the Rebels will circle around behind and attack our lines from both sides. This is it, men."

Turn the page.

Soon, you hear a high-pitched wailing called the Rebel yell. The Confederates are attacking. An officer runs toward you. "I need reinforcement on the left flank," he shouts at you, George, and several nearby soldiers. The officer points to a spot about 50 feet down the line.

"I'll go, sir," George replies.

"George!" you say once the officer is out of earshot. "You're putting yourself right in the line of fire."

George shrugs and slings his rifle over his shoulder. "I came here to fight. You coming with me or not?"

➺ To stay where you are, go to page 47.

➺ To join George on the flank, turn to page 48.

"Good luck," you tell George, shaking his hand. "I'm going to take my chances here."

You watch George take his position as you take cover behind a boulder. You can't see very far. The shouts of the advancing Rebels are getting louder. The sound of gunshots is deafening.

Before you know it, the first attack is upon you. You take careful, well-aimed shots. You see a Confederate officer and fire. The officer spins and falls as your shot hits him in the shoulder.

Out of the corner of your eye, you see George. He's been hit! His right arm is bleeding, and his rifle has fallen from his grasp. He's lying right in the line of fire.

➤ To get up to help your friend, turn to page **49**.

➤ To hold your position, turn to page **50**.

"Okay, I'm with you," you answer. You and George walk to the end of the Union line.

As you take your place, waves of gray and brown Confederate uniforms pour out of the woods. You take aim and fire. A Rebel soldier falls to the ground, screaming. While you reload, several Confederates charge at you and George. As they take aim, you pull George to the ground. An enemy shot whizzes overhead, right where you had just been standing.

From your knees, you take aim again. You see a Confederate soldier out in the open. But he's on the ground, holding his leg. Farther back, you see a Rebel officer urging his men on in the attack. It will be a tough shot to hit him from such a distance, but he seems like the bigger threat.

❧ To take the shot at the officer, turn to page **52**.

❧ To take the shot at the soldier, turn to page **58**.

"George!" you shout, running. Shots whiz past as you stand up. George sees you coming and stumbles to get up. You can only watch in horror as another shot hits him square in the gut. He slumps to the ground.

"No!" you scream as you rush to his side, barely aware of the danger. Another shot whistles by, so close that you can almost feel it.

George is pale and cool by the time you reach him. "Tell my wife that I love her," he whispers.

"Hold on," you tell him, trying to help him up. If you can get George to the rear of the line, he might make it. But he's fighting you.

"No," he coughs. "Get yourself back to cover." You know that he's right. You'll be safer if you stay low. But unless you can move him, George will die — and soon.

❧ *To get back behind cover, turn to page* **50**.

❧ *To move George to safety, turn to page* **69**.

You feel helpless, knowing there's nothing you can do for your friend. But helping him now would be almost certain death. You duck behind a boulder.

A nearby shot quickly focuses your attention back to the attacking Confederates. You slowly raise your rifle and squeeze off a single shot. A Confederate soldier drops to the ground.

The battle rages on. Smoke rolls across the battlefield. Eventually, the Confederates retreat. Taking deep, heavy breaths, you wipe the sweat from your face. You can't see George anymore, but you know he must be dead. There's no time to mourn your friend, though. Before long, the Confederates will be back.

The Confederates charge again, fighting bravely. But you and your regiment have the high ground. Once again, you force them to retreat.

Soldiers on Little Round Top took shelter behind large boulders.

"Save your ammunition, men!" shouts the colonel. You check your supply. You started with 60 rounds. There are only six shots left.

The man to your right looks at you. You recognize him as John, your neighbor from back home. "I'm out," he says. "Quick, give me some of your ammunition before they come again."

➤ To give John the ammunition, turn to page **54**.

➤ To keep your ammunition, turn to page **60**.

The 20th Maine used bayonets to force the Confederates to retreat.

You take aim at the officer and gently squeeze the trigger. The officer jumps as the shot whizzes by. You missed, but it doesn't matter. Within moments, the Rebels are retreating. You and George join in the cheering as the regiment celebrates the victory. "We did it!" you shout.

"No, that was just the first attack. They'll be back," George answers.

Sure enough, the Rebels attack again and again. Soon, you're out of ammunition. So is George and most of the regiment.

"Bayonet!" shouts Colonel Chamberlain. You take the long, sharp blade and secure it to the front of your rifle.

The regiment stands and rushes down to meet the Confederates. They're surprised by the move, giving the Union soldiers an advantage. Before you have a chance to get in on the action, the Rebels are in full retreat. This time, with sunset quickly approaching, there's real cause for celebration. You've held the line.

Not far from you, a Confederate soldier is stumbling away in retreat. He's limping badly, and you know you could catch him. You run at the fleeing soldier. He sees you coming and raises a rifle in your direction.

→ To try to take the soldier prisoner, turn to page **56**.

→ To let him go, turn to page **57**.

"Here. Don't waste them," you say as you hand three precious cartridges to John. You have just enough time to get a drink of water before the battle is on again. The Rebels are coming closer than ever, determined to break through the line.

The attack is shockingly swift. You fire a shot and then another. The Rebels keep coming closer and closer. An enemy shot hits the boulder in front of you. "Get down," shouts John. You duck, and he fires a shot over your head. It hits an enemy soldier who had been aiming right at you.

"Now, aren't you glad you gave me some ammunition?" John asks you.

Together, you reload and fire one last shot. Your ammunition is gone, and you're not the only one. The regiment has all but run out. How will you stop the Rebel advance?

"Bayonet!" shouts Colonel Chamberlain. You take the long, sharp blade and secure it to the front of your rifle.

You move away from the safety of the boulder and rush downhill with your regiment. The counterattack surprises the Rebel troops. In moments, you're in the thick of the battle. Out of the corner of your eye, you spot a Confederate officer in front of you. He's aiming a pistol right at Colonel Chamberlain.

→ To try to kill the officer with your bayonet, turn to page **62**.

→ To try to tackle him instead, turn to page **63**.

"He's bluffing," you think, hoping he's out of ammunition as well. You take a few more steps and watch as he slowly lowers his rifle. You were right. You raise your bayonet and shout for the soldier to surrender. He holds up his empty hands and allows you to take him.

"Come with me," you say gruffly.

You march the man back behind the Union line, turning him over to a sergeant. Maybe the man will have information about the Rebel plans. And if not, at least he won't be able to attack again. He'll be sent to a prison camp to wait out the rest of the war.

"Good work, private," Colonel Chamberlain tells you, putting his hand on your shoulder. "You should feel proud of what you've done today."

Turn to page 67.

The battlefield of Gettysburg was crowded and filled with confusion.

You and the Confederate soldier stare at each other for several moments. You can see in his eyes that he is as tired as you are. He looks like a young man, but there are already gray streaks in his full beard.

Both of you lower your weapons at the same time. Without taking his eyes off you, the Confederate takes a careful step backward. You do the same, nodding. The man turns and runs down the hill. You turn and rejoin your regiment. The fighting is over, at least for today.

Turn to page 67.

You take aim at the wounded Rebel soldier and squeeze the trigger. The man is thrown backward as the shot slams into his chest. Meanwhile, George takes a shot at the officer. He misses, and the Rebels keep coming.

As you reload, George shouts, "Get down!" As you turn to look, you feel a strange sensation in your stomach. You drop your rifle and run your hand along the front of your uniform. It's slick with blood.

George fires a shot, then ducks down. "A gut shot. Hold on," he says over the gunfire. He grabs your loaded rifle and fires it.

"They're falling back!" he tells you. You can hear the whooping and shouting of your regiment. George shouts for help. As you begin to lose consciousness, other soldiers carry you off the field.

Doctors and nurses set up field hospitals in tents near battlefields.

You wake up in a field hospital. You overhear the low voice of a doctor nearby. "There's nothing I can do for him," he says. You know he's talking about you.

For three days, you drift in and out of consciousness. A shot to the stomach is one of the slowest and most painful ways to die. When death finally comes, you welcome it.

THE END

To follow another path, turn to page 11.
To read the conclusion, turn to page 101.

"Find someone else," you answer. "I don't have enough."

John scowls and moves down the line, asking for ammunition. A short time later, the Rebels charge again. The attack is even more furious than the earlier charges. Gray and brown uniforms are everywhere. As you fire a shot into the madness, splinters of wood from a nearby tree shatter into the air.

Moments later, a bullet catches you in the left arm. The force of it throws you back several feet. Your head cracks against a boulder, and you lose consciousness.

The next thing you remember, you're lying in a crowded field hospital. The sounds of wounded and dying men fill the air. Weakly, you call for help. You feel a hand on your shoulder as a doctor looks at your wound.

"Sorry, son, but this arm will have to go," the doctor tells you. He puts a cloth over your mouth and tells you to inhale. The fumes cause you to drift out of consciousness. You know that when you awake, your left arm will be gone.

You've survived the bloodiest battle of the war, but you've paid a heavy price. The stump at the end of your left shoulder will always remind you of your part in the battle of Gettysburg.

THE END

To follow another path, turn to page 11.
To read the conclusion, turn to page 101.

In a rage, you run at the Confederate officer. Just as he's about to shoot, you thrust your bayonet into his belly. Surprised, he turns. His dark brown eyes stare into yours. He stumbles, raises the pistol, and fires.

At first, you're not sure what's happened. Then you feel it. You've been shot in the chest. Air rushes from your lungs as you lift your hand to the wound. Together, you and the officer fall to the ground, eyes still locked.

"It's a good death," he whispers. The darkness is creeping in all around you. All you can do is nod.

You die on the field of Gettysburg, your head resting on the body of the Confederate you killed. Your last thought is, "Was it all worth it?"

THE END

To follow another path, turn to page 11.
To read the conclusion, turn to page 101.

You shout as you slam into the officer. He sprawls to the ground, his pistol flying out of his grasp. He quickly gets up, turns around, and runs away. His fellow Confederates soon follow. You've done it! You've beaten back the Rebel charge once again.

The field is littered with bodies and blood. In the confusing aftermath, you find George's body and say a prayer.

As night closes in, you and your fellow soldiers fall into an exhausted sleep. You wake with a start when you hear Colonel Chamberlain's voice. "Boys, we've been asked to occupy that hill in front," he says, pointing in the darkness in the direction of Big Round Top. "Do I have some volunteers?"

Turn the page.

Union troops retreated to Cemetery Hill on July 1. The hill was also the site of heavy fighting on July 2 and 3.

You try to shake off the sleep as you rise to your feet. Looking around, you see all the other soldiers on their feet too. With only the full moon as a guide, you make your way quietly up Big Round Top. You spend the night half-asleep behind a boulder, waiting for the sun to rise.

Early the next morning, July 3, you and the other soldiers build a stone wall for protection. About 1:00 in the afternoon, you hear a loud thundering noise. The battle is in full swing again, about a mile north of your regiment's protected position.

After two hours, the shelling ends. The silence is eerie. You slowly move away from the stone wall as the news spreads.

You learn Lee attacked the heart of the Union line at a place called Cemetery Ridge. Major General George Pickett and his Virginia soldiers led about 12,000 Confederate troops across an open field separating the lines. It was a last, desperate charge. The Union soldiers were ready for them, with plenty of reinforcements. By late afternoon, more than half of the Confederate soldiers are dead, wounded, or captured.

Turn the page.

The battle is an important but costly Union victory. You hear that about 23,000 Union soldiers are dead, injured, or missing. The Confederate losses were even greater, with about 28,000 dead, injured, or missing soldiers.

You think about George and the other brave men who died on both sides. You wonder if there were really any winners in this bloody battle.

THE END

To follow another path, turn to page 11.
To read the conclusion, turn to page 101.

Confederate General Lewis Armistead (top, right) led his brigade during Pickett's Charge.

The Union forces regroup as night falls. Your regiment is reassigned to defend Big Round Top. You spend the night huddled against a boulder on the hill. Early the next morning, your regiment builds a stone wall for protection. You stay behind the wall most of the day. The heavy fighting is about a mile to your north.

That afternoon, Lee orders a charge at the very heart of the Union line, at a place called Cemetery Ridge. It's a last, desperate attack.

Turn the page.

The Union army is ready. Cannons boom as the brave Confederate soldiers try to cross an open field. The attack is doomed, and soon the Confederates are driven back.

"I can't believe they charged," George says when it's over. "General Lee should have fallen back and regrouped."

"Is the war over?" you ask. "Can the Rebels recover from this defeat?

"It's far from over," George answers. "We hurt them badly here. But they'll keep fighting."

"So will we," you say. You look down at the smoldering battlefield. The bodies of soldiers from both sides are scattered everywhere. It's a Union victory, but a costly one. The war will go on. You just hope you live to see the end of it.

THE END

To follow another path, turn to page 11.
To read the conclusion, turn to page 101.

"Never," you tell your friend. "I'm not giving up on you." But even as you say the words, you see your friend's face growing paler.

You hook your arm under George's shoulder and around his back. He moans weakly as you lift him from the ground. The sounds of gunfire fill the air. You hear something whiz past your ear.

Suddenly, you feel a strange tingling in your side. The strength in your legs gives out. You've been hit! The two of you collapse to the ground as the fight rages on. Instantly, you know it's bad. When you put your hand to your side, it's stained bright red with blood.

"Sorry, friend," George whispers to you, just before his eyes close one last time. You're sad you won't live to see the end of the battle. But at least you'll die with your best friend at your side.

THE END

To follow another path, turn to page 11.
To read the conclusion, turn to page 101.

Union gunboats shelled Vicksburg from the Mississippi River during the siege.

CHAPTER 4

LIVING UNDER SIEGE

A low, rumbling sound fills the air. It sounds like thunder, but you know that it's really Union cannons. They boom night and day, shelling your beloved city of Vicksburg, Mississippi.

You hold tightly to the hand of your sister, Anna. She's only 12 years old — six years younger than you. With your mother dead and your father serving in the Confederate army, you're all the family she has. You have almost become used to the shelling over the past weeks, but that doesn't make it any less terrifying. You miss your husband, who is off serving with the Confederate army. You'd been married only a few weeks before he had to leave for war.

71

Turn the page.

You never thought it would come to this. In May, Confederate soldiers fought off two Union attacks. Then, Union General Ulysses S. Grant ordered a siege of Vicksburg. He's blocking supplies from entering the city and trying to blast it into surrender. With its location on the Mississippi River, Vicksburg is important to the Confederate defense. If the city falls, the Union will take a big step toward choking off an already undersupplied Confederate army. General John Pemberton commands the 20,000 soldiers who defend the city from the much larger Union force.

The shelling is getting closer. A house not far from your own was hit last night.

"It's getting too dangerous to stay here, even if we hide in the cellar," Anna reminds you. "Almost all of the other women and children have fled to the caves."

Union soldiers also took shelter in dugouts on Vicksburg's hillsides.

You know that she's right. Few people have died during the shelling, but thousands have taken shelter in caves dug in the hills near the city. But you don't want to leave your home. The thought of living in the cold, damp caves seems almost too terrible to bear.

⋗ To stay in your home, turn to page 74.

⋗ To take shelter in the caves, turn to page 79.

"We're not leaving our home," you tell Anna. "There isn't a safe place in this city right now. At least here, we've got a little food and comfortable beds."

The Union navy joins the army in shelling the city. You stay in the cellar that night. The booming of cannon fire makes sleep impossible. But at least you're at home.

Just before dawn, you hear a scratching sound from above. Carefully, you climb the cellar stairs. You hear voices from inside the pantry. Thieves! They're stealing what little food you've got!

The thieves don't know that you're there. Who knows what they might do if you call out. Do they have guns? Are they so hungry that they'd kill for a few bags of flour? But if you do nothing, what will you and Anna eat?

You decide that confronting the thieves is too dangerous. Maybe someone outside could help. Or maybe you should sneak back down into the cellar and wait for them to leave. You can deal with hunger. You can't deal with facing a shotgun or pistol.

➤ To sneak back down to the cellar, turn to page 76.

➤ To run into the street and call for help, turn to page 77.

As quietly as you can, you sneak back into the cellar and lock yourself inside. You know that all of your food will be gone, but at least you and Anna will be safe. After a few minutes, the sounds from upstairs stop. The thieves have left, but you're not about to go back up there until the sun is up.

In the morning, your fears are confirmed. The thieves took almost all of your food. Strangely, they didn't bother taking any valuables. You were sure at least your silverware would be gone.

When Anna gets up, you break the bad news. "I hate to do it, but it's just not safe here," you tell her. "We have no choice left but to go to the caves."

Turn to page 79.

You dash outside into the street.

"Help!" you cry. "I'm being robbed!"

Your voice echoes up and down the street. There's not a soul to be seen. Most of your neighbors have moved to the caves.

From inside, you hear scrambling noises. The thieves have heard you. What if they're coming outside to get you? You dart to the side of the house and hide behind some shrubs. You hear the house's back door slam shut. "Let's get out of here," whispers a man. "General Pemberton will have our heads if he finds out about this."

You realize with horror that the thieves are Confederate soldiers! The thought gives you a chill. The very men who are supposed to be protecting you are now stealing from you.

Turn the page.

The sound of hurried footsteps slowly fades away. You wait in your hiding spot for several minutes before going back inside. You tiptoe into the house and light a lamp. One look in the pantry shows you that the thieves made off with almost all of your food.

You're furious. The thieves had mentioned General John Pemberton, the commander of the Confederate army defending Vicksburg. Should you report the incident to the Confederate officers? Or would it be just a waste of time?

➻ To go to General Pemberton's headquarters to report the theft, turn to page **85**.

➻ To drop the matter and go in search of food, turn to page **88**.

Many people often gathered in one small cave during the siege.

"Let's go," you say with a sigh.

You and Anna quickly pack a few things. You take what little food you have. You each bring a change of clothes, blankets, and a few small valuables.

The city streets are all but deserted as you make your way to the caves. Small cooking fires burn outside the caves as you look for a spot to settle. Thin, exhausted faces watch you. Almost all of them are women, children, and the elderly.

Turn the page.

"This won't be so bad," you say hopefully, though you really don't believe it.

The caves are bustling with activity. Several slaves are cooking soup in large pots above ground. As you and Anna settle into a small dugout, you spread the blankets over the dirt floor. At least you'll have a place to sleep.

One of Anna's school friends, Edward, sees you and comes running over. "Hi, Anna!" he says excitedly. "Did you hear? General Pemberton has asked civilians to search for unexploded Yankee shells. Our soldiers need the gunpowder inside. Do you want to help me find some?"

Anna looks at you, her eyes bright with interest. You can tell she wants to go. But going out to look for shells could be dangerous.

To agree to look for shells, go to page **81**.

To refuse, turn to page **83**.

"I guess we should do our part to help the army," you say reluctantly. "But it will be dark soon. Let's go in the morning."

"Great!" says Edward. Sure enough, he's back at dawn, ready to go. The three of you make your way out into the abandoned city streets. You see a few other people searching, but nobody has found anything.

Suddenly, Edward shouts. He's found a large unexploded mortar shell. The three of you stand looking at it. "It's going to be heavy," Edward says. "Help me carry it."

"Wait," you say, hesitant. You know how powerful this weapon is. Suddenly, you don't want anything to do with it. "Maybe we should just tell a soldier where it is."

Turn the page.

The Confederate army had a large arsenal of weapons at Vicksburg.

"Don't be silly," Edward says, sighing. "This is what we came out here to do. The army needs the gunpowder. Now are you going to help me or not?"

→ To help Edward pick up the shell, turn to page **90**.

→ To back away, turn to page **97**.

You give Anna a sharp look and shake your head. "Sorry, Edward, but I think we'd rather stay where we're safe."

The boy frowns and shrugs his shoulders. "All right, then," he says, and wanders off.

"We should have helped," Anna says. "What are we going to do here? Just sit around and feel sorry for ourselves?"

You sigh. "I'm just too hungry to do anything," you answer. "Tomorrow we have to find some more food."

A woman in a nearby dugout motions for you to come over. She is thin and pale and looks very tired. With a shock, you recognize her as your mother's old friend, Clara. She appears to have aged 20 years since the spring.

Turn the page.

"I'm so glad to see you two," Clara says, giving Anna a big hug. "Come, you must be hungry. My servant is making some supper. It's not much, but you're welcome to eat with us."

"Oh, thank you," you say, finally managing a genuine smile. The thought of a hot meal sounds wonderful. A few minutes later, a young slave girl brings down a pot filled with some sort of stew. The girl fills three bowls and hands them to you, Anna, and Clara.

"What is it?" Anna asks.

"Better not to ask," Clara replies.

Anna makes a face. "It's rat, isn't it?"

"Meat is meat," Clara says, "and the two of you need the energy. Now eat up."

➤ *To eat the rat soup, turn to page **91**.*

➤ *To refuse, turn to page **93**.*

You take Anna by the hand and march down to the general's headquarters. A young soldier greets you, and you explain what has happened.

The soldier's face darkens. "It's certainly possible, ma'am. But I don't know what I can do if you can't identify the men."

"Will you tell the general?" you ask.

"No, the general has a lot on his mind. He doesn't need to know about every little problem."

Just then, you hear heavy footsteps. "What don't I need to know, sergeant?"

To your shock, there stands General John Pemberton himself. Northern-born, he doesn't speak with the familiar Southern accent. You explain what happened and why you think it was Confederate soldiers who robbed you.

Turn the page.

General John Pemberton commanded Confederate forces at Vicksburg.

Pemberton breathes a long, heavy sigh. "I'm sorry, ma'am. Our men only get some flour, cowpeas, and a bit of bacon each day. They're hungry. Some are getting desperate."

"So what will you do?" you ask.

Pemberton looks at the young soldier. "Have the quartermaster give these ladies a bag of flour," he orders. "I'm sorry it's not more," he adds, turning to you. "We haven't much to spare. I'd advise you to go to the caves. Your home is not a safe place to stay. Good day, ladies."

Sadly, you agree. The house just isn't safe anymore. You and Anna pack a few clothes, blankets, and valuables and make your way to the caves.

Turn to page 99.

There's no point in reporting the theft. After all, you can't even identify the thieves. You and Anna take the little money you have left and head into the city. You hope to find some beef or pork, but nobody has any for sale.

"I have mule meat and dog meat for sale," cracks the voice of an old man across the street. "Interested?" His eyes gleam greedily.

"How much for the mule?" you ask.

"Five dollars," he replies.

"Five dollars?" you gasp. "We can't afford that."

"Two dollars for the dog, then." Anna looks at you with horror. "We can't eat dog," she insists.

You don't have a lot of choices. You can either buy the dog meat or trap rats for food. Neither idea is very appealing.

➤ To refuse the man's offer, go to page 89.

➤ To buy the dog meat, turn to page 95.

"No thank you, sir. Good day," you answer. You take Anna by the hand and stomp away.

The two of you make it back home before you break down in tears. "What are we going to do?" you ask.

"I'd rather eat rats than dog," Anna says.

You nod slowly. "Come on, let's go inside," you say. But just as you stand up, a shell crashes into the house next door. Wood splinters and glass shatters. You both throw yourselves to the ground, covering your ears.

The house is destroyed. Luckily, nobody has been living there for more than a week. The family who owns it fled to the caves. You know that you have to do the same.

Quickly, you pack a few things and hurry down to the caves. You'd hoped to avoid it, but there's just no other choice.

Turn to page 99.

Edward is right. You need to get this shell to the trenches where the Confederate defenders are dug in.

"All right," you say, slowly approaching the shell. "But Anna, you stay back. Edward and I can handle this."

Scowling, Anna steps back. You and Edward stand over the shell and work your hands beneath it. "On three," he says. "One, two . . . three!" Together, you lift the shell to waist height. Edward smiles, saying "See, that wasn't so . . ."

Boom!

The shell explodes, sending fragments of metal flying in all directions. The violent explosion kills both you and Edward before you even realize what happened.

THE END

To follow another path, turn to page 11.
To read the conclusion, turn to page 101.

With a sigh, you take the soup and lift a spoonful to your lips. In truth, there's very little meat in it. You can almost fool yourself into believing that it's chicken.

As the siege continues, you and Anna do all you can to survive. Soon, the thought of eating rat isn't even disgusting anymore. It's just the way things are. Once in awhile, if you're lucky, you get a piece of mule meat or corn bread.

Soon, clean water is almost as scarce as food. You wait in line for a single bucket. There's no water for bathing, and the caves smell of old, musty sweat.

The shelling continues. Nothing General Pemberton and the Confederate army do seems to matter. On July 3, the rumor that Pemberton will surrender swirls through the caves. You can't decide whether you're sad or relieved.

Turn the page.

The surrender formally happens on Independence Day, July 4. Soon, you and Anna return to your home, which has suffered only minor damage. Before long, life is almost back to normal.

The fall of Vicksburg is a terrible blow to the Confederate army. You hope the war will end soon. Maybe then your husband will return home and life can go on. You just pray he's still alive.

THE END

To follow another path, turn to page 11.
To read the conclusion, turn to page 101.

"Rat? You can't be serious," you say, handing the bowl back to Clara. "I'll never be hungry enough to eat vermin!"

You grab Anna's arm, causing her to spill her soup. "But I'm hungry," she cries as you drag her back to your dugout.

That night, you use a little of the flour you have left to make biscuits. The hard biscuits taste terrible and do little to fill your growling stomachs. Anna cries herself to sleep. You lie awake for hours, trying to ignore your hunger pangs.

After a few days, Anna decides to eat rat. But you never change your mind. You survive by eating any other scrap of food you can find. An old, rotten apple is like a treasure.

Turn the page.

Some civilians were hurt or killed by Union shells that missed their mark.

Soon you're too weak to leave the caves. You're lying down one day when a shell blasts into the ground above you. The cave ceiling gives way, dumping tons of rock on top of you.

Your dying thought is of Anna. You pray she'll do what you couldn't — survive the terrible siege of Vicksburg.

THE END

To follow another path, turn to page 11.
To read the conclusion, turn to page 101.

You hand the man the money. He gives you a slab of foul-smelling meat wrapped in old newspaper.

That night, you cook some of the meat, adding lots of spices in hopes you can forget what you're eating. Anna still refuses to eat the dog, but you choke it down. It tastes rotten. Less than an hour after you eat it, you're vomiting.

You feel weaker and weaker as the evening goes on. Anna helps you to bed, where you sleep restlessly. The next day, you're suffering from terrible diarrhea. You keep trying to vomit, but there's nothing left in your stomach. You feel burning hot one minute and cold the next.

The next thing you remember, an old doctor is standing over your bed. Anna is next to him, looking worried.

Turn the page.

It's days before you're well enough to get out of bed. Even then, you feel too weak to do anything. The shelling continues, and you realize that your house isn't safe. A few of your neighbors come over from the caves to help you and Anna move.

You spend several long, miserable weeks in the caves. On July 4, General Pemberton and the Confederate army surrender the city to General Grant's forces.

When you return home, your strength still hasn't returned. Anna, almost skeleton thin from the weeks of hunger, has to do the housework. You've survived the siege, but your body has paid a heavy price. You'll never be strong again.

THE END

To follow another path, turn to page 11.
To read the conclusion, turn to page 101.

"No, this doesn't feel right, Edward. Let's leave it alone."

Edward frowns. "That's what I get for going shell hunting with a couple of girls," he says. "I'll bring it back myself."

He bends over to lift the shell. "Don't!" you shout as you and Anna back up. Boom! The shell explodes as Edward lifts it. The sound is deafening. You scream as you're thrown to the ground. Anna is sobbing. "Edward's dead! He's dead!" she wails.

A small crowd gathers, rushing you and Anna away from the scene. A small piece of the shell hit your arm, and it's bleeding heavily. Back in the caves, an old woman tends to your wound. She serves you and Anna a thin, foul-tasting soup that you both eat without question. You realize that the little scraps of meat in the soup are rat, but you're too exhausted to care.

Turn the page.

On July 4, 1863, Grant's soldiers entered Vicksburg after Pemberton's surrender.

You and Anna survive by eating rat, mule, and whatever else you can find. On July 4, General Pemberton finally surrenders. The Yankees take control of the city. It's not the way you hoped it would end, but at least you can get food and clean water again.

You know the memory of young Edward will haunt you forever, but at least you're alive.

THE END

To follow another path, turn to page 11.
To read the conclusion, turn to page 101.

The caves are crawling with people. You and Anna find a small dugout and try to make it feel like home. The place smells terrible. Nobody has water to spare for bathing. The sounds of coughing and crying keep you up at night. It's a terrible way to live.

Anna adjusts better than you do. She proves to be an excellent rat trapper. The first time you cook and eat a rat, you both vomit. But after awhile, you get used to the idea and the taste. It's food, after all.

On July 4, General Pemberton surrenders. The Yankees take control of the city. You and Anna finally return home. But you know life in the South will never be the same.

THE END

To follow another path, turn to page 11.
To read the conclusion, turn to page 101.

President Lincoln (center) is shown with detective Allan Pinkerton (left) and General John McClernand (right) after the Battle of Antietam.

CHAPTER 5

THE TIDE TURNS

The Civil War was long and bloody. Early in the war, the Confederacy held the advantage. Confederate soldiers defeated the Union troops in battle after battle. Their victories included the first and second Battles of Bull Run and the Seven Days' Battles.

The Union army did have some success early on, including the bloody Battle of Antietam. Yet by the end of 1862, Confederate independence seemed like a real possibility. Northerners were tired of the war. Support for President Lincoln was fading. Many people believed political pressure could force the Union to give the Confederacy the independence it wanted.

The events of the spring and summer of 1863 were a turning point in the war. The change may have begun at Chancellorsville. Even though the Confederates won the battle, General Stonewall Jackson was killed. Jackson had been General Lee's most trusted officer. Without him, the Confederate army was never the same.

The loss of Jackson was strongly felt at Gettysburg. Lee lacked confidence in some of his generals. The Confederates failed to take the high ground that was so important to the battle. When General George Meade's force stopped Lee's final, desperate charge, the Union had the victory it so badly needed.

The fall of Vicksburg was even more important than Gettysburg. The Union then controlled the Mississippi River, splitting the Confederacy in two.

Union General William Sherman led the March to the Sea through Georgia.

The losses at Gettysburg and Vicksburg were a huge blow to the Confederates. Even so, they fought bravely for the next two years. The Confederacy had a few victories, but the Union had greater supplies and many more soldiers.

In 1864, Union General William Tecumseh Sherman captured the important railroad and factory town of Atlanta, Georgia. He then led his troops on a march through Georgia to Savannah. When Lincoln was elected again in 1864, the Confederacy's hopes were all but gone.

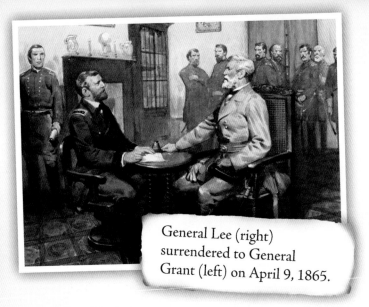

General Lee (right) surrendered to General Grant (left) on April 9, 1865.

After Vicksburg, Lincoln finally found the general he'd been looking for in Ulysses Grant. Grant had the confidence earlier Union generals had lacked. He wasn't afraid to attack, even if it meant losing men.

On April 9, 1865, Lee and Grant met in a small Virginia village called Appomattox Court House. There, Lee surrendered his army. In the following weeks, the other Confederate armies also surrendered. After four years of brutal, bloody war, it was over.

The Civil War left scars that lasted generations. Slavery ended, but life didn't improve greatly for African Americans. They were treated as second-class citizens for another 100 years, especially in the South. After the war, the federal government stepped in to govern the former Confederacy. This Reconstruction period lasted until 1877, when Southern states were again allowed to govern themselves.

The Civil War was perhaps the darkest time in American history. Neighbors, friends, and brothers fought against one another. More than 600,000 people died. But even with the problems the war caused, the country stayed together. We can only imagine how different our lives would be without the events of 1863.

Time Line

December 1860–June 1861 — Eleven Southern states secede from the Union to form the Confederate States of America.

April 12, 1861 — The Confederacy attacks Fort Sumter, South Carolina, beginning the Civil War.

July 21, 1861 — The Confederacy wins the war's first major battle at Bull Run, Virginia.

April 6–7, 1862 — The Union wins the Battle of Shiloh in Tennessee.

June 25–July 1, 1862 — The Confederacy wins the Seven Days' Battles near Richmond, Virginia.

September 17, 1862 — The Union wins the Battle of Antietam in Maryland.

May 1, 1863 — The heavy fighting of the Battle of Chancellorsville begins.

May 2, 1863 — General Stonewall Jackson is shot accidentally by his own troops.

May 6, 1863 — Union troops make their final retreat from Chancellorsville, giving the Confederacy the victory.

May 10, 1863 — Stonewall Jackson dies.

May 1863 — General Ulysses S. Grant begins the siege of Vicksburg.

July 1, 1863 — The Union and Confederate armies meet at Gettysburg.

July 3, 1863 — The final Confederate charge at Gettysburg fails; the Union wins the battle.

July 4, 1863 — General John Pemberton surrenders the city of Vicksburg to General Grant.

November 8, 1864 — President Lincoln is re-elected.

November 15, 1864 — General William Sherman begins his March to the Sea in Atlanta, Georgia.

December 10, 1864 — General Sherman's march reaches Savannah, Georgia. Savannah surrenders 11 days later.

April 9, 1865 — General Lee surrenders to General Grant at Appomattox Court House, Virginia.

April 15, 1865 — President Lincoln dies after being shot the evening before in Washington, D.C.

December 1865 — The 13th Amendment to the Constitution outlaws slavery in the United States.

1865 – 1877 — The federal government takes over Southern state governments; this period is called Reconstruction.

OTHER PATHS
TO EXPLORE

In this book, you've seen how the events experienced by people during the Civil War look different from three points of view.

Perspectives on history are as varied as the people who lived it. You can explore other paths on your own to learn more about what happened. Seeing history from many points of view is an important part of understanding it.

Here are some ideas for other Civil War points of view to explore:

- ✦ Late in the war, many Southern families along Sherman's march feared that their homes would be burned down. What would that have been like?

- ✦ Friends and family members often fought on opposite sides. What would it have been like to meet a close friend, or even a brother, as an enemy on the battlefield?

- ✦ Some African Americans fought for the Union, but they were treated as second-class soldiers. What was the war like for them?

READ MORE

Koestler-Grack, Rachel A. *Stonewall Jackson.* New York: Chelsea House, 2009.

Landau, Elaine. *The Battle of Gettysburg: Would You Lead the Fight?* Berkeley Heights, N.J.: Enslow Elementary, 2009.

Lassieur, Allison. *The Battle of Bull Run: An Interactive History Adventure.* Mankato, Minn.: Capstone Press, 2009.

Rebman, Renée C. *The Union Soldier.* Minneapolis: Compass Point Books, 2007.

INTERNET SITES

FactHound offers a safe, fun way to find Internet sites related to this book. All of the sites on FactHound have been researched by our staff.

Here's all you do:

Visit *www.facthound.com*

FactHound will fetch the best sites for you!

GLOSSARY

bayonet (BAY-uh-net) — a long metal blade attached to the end of a musket or rifle

cavalry (KA-vuhl-ree) — soldiers who travel and fight on horseback

cellar (SEL-ur) — a basement

court-martial (KORT-mar-shuhl) — a military trial

deserter (di-ZURT-ur) — a military member who leaves duty without permission

flank (FLANK) — the right or left of a military formation

rebel (REB-uhl) — a person who fights against a government; Confederate soldiers were called Rebels during the Civil War.

Reconstruction (ree-kuhn-STRUHKT-shuhn) — the period of time following the Civil War when the U.S. government tried to rebuild Southern states

regiment (REJ-uh-muhnt) — a large group of soldiers who fight together as a unit

siege (SEEJ) — the surrounding of a city to cut off supplies and then wait for those inside to surrender

Yankee (YANG-kee) — a nickname for Union soldiers during the Civil War

BIBLIOGRAPHY

Barton, Michael, and Larry M. Logue, eds. *The Civil War Soldier: A Historical Reader.* New York: New York University Press, 2002.

Catton, Bruce. *The American Heritage New History of the Civil War.* New York: Viking, 1996.

The Civil War — A Film by Ken Burns
http://www.pbs.org/civilwar

The Civil War Home Page
http://www.civil-war.net

Gallman, J. Matthew, ed. *The Civil War Chronicle.* New York: Crown Publishers, 2000.

Hoehling, A. A. *Vicksburg: 47 Days of Siege.* Mechanicsburg, Pa.: Stackpole Books, 1996.

Symonds, Craig L. *American Heritage History of the Battle of Gettysburg.* New York: HarperCollins, 2001.

Volo, Dorothy Denneen, and James M. Volo. *Daily Life in Civil War America.* Westport, Conn.: Greenwood Press, 1998.

Wagner, Margaret E., Gary W. Gallagher, and Paul Finkelman, eds. *The Library of Congress Civil War Desk Reference.* New York: Simon & Schuster, 2002.

INDEX